D1621022

The Last Week in the Life of Christ

NELSON/REGENCY

Nashville

�֍ �֍ ✷ ✷ ✷ ✷ ✷ ✷ ✷ ✷ ✷ ✷ ✷ ✷ ✷

Contents

❀❀❀❀❀❀❀❀❀❀❀❀❀❀❀❀❀❀

❀ ❀ ❀ ❀ ❀ ❀ ❀ ❀ ❀ ❀ ❀ ❀ ❀ ❀ ❀

Introduction

Jesus said, "Now My soul is troubled, and what shall I say? 'Father, save Me from this hour'? But for this purpose I came to this hour. Father, glorify Your name" (John 12:27, 28).

Jesus made a decision to go through this final week of life on earth, because He believed that humankind was worth it. He knew that unless He died, we could never really live—not the way God had intended for us to—free from bondage and confusion. He said, "Unless a grain of wheat falls into the ground and dies, it remains alone; but if

❄ ❄ ❄ ❄ ❄ ❄ ❄ ❄ ❄ ❄ ❄ ❄ ❄ ❄ ❄

it dies, it produces much grain" (John 12:24). He willingly became the "grain of wheat."

❄   ❄   ❄

As you are reading these scripture accounts of events in this final week of Jesus' life, remember that the Jewish day was from sunset to sunset. For example, Friday actually began on what we consider Thursday evening. This will help you picture more clearly the events of this vitally important week.

Sunday

❀ ❀ ❀ ❀ ❀ ❀ ❀ ❀ ❀ ❀ ❀ ❀ ❀ ❀ ❀

THE TRIUMPHAL ENTRY
Mark 11

1

Now when they drew near Jerusalem, to Bethphage and Bethany, at the Mount of Olives, He sent two of His disciples;

2

and He said to them, "Go into the village opposite you; and as soon as you have entered it you will find a

❀ ❀ ❀ ❀ ❀ ❀ ❀ ❀ ❀ ❀ ❀ ❀ ❀ ❀

colt tied, on which no one has sat.
Loose it and bring it.

3

"And if anyone says to you, 'Why
are you doing this?' say, 'The Lord
has need of it,' and immediately he
will send it here."

4

So they went their way, and found
the colt tied by the door outside on
the street, and they loosed it.

❋ ❋ ❋ ❋ ❋ ❋ ❋ ❋ ❋ ❋ ❋ ❋ ❋ ❋ ❋

5

But some of those who stood there said to them, "What are you doing, loosing the colt?"

6

And they spoke to them just as Jesus had commanded. So they let them go.

7

Then they brought the colt to Jesus and threw their clothes on it, and He sat on it.

8

And many spread their clothes on the road, and others cut down leafy branches from the trees and spread them on the road.

9

Then those who went before and those who followed cried out, saying:

"Hosanna!
'Blessed is He who comes in the name of the LORD!'

❊ ❊ ❊ ❊ ❊ ❊ ❊ ❊ ❊ ❊ ❊ ❊ ❊ ❊ ❊

10

Blessed is the kingdom of our
* father David*
That comes in the name of the
* Lord!*
Hosanna in the highest!''

11

And Jesus went into Jerusalem and
into the temple. So when He had
looked around at all things, as the
hour was already late, He went out
to Bethany with the twelve.

Monday

❊ ❊ ❊ ❊ ❊ ❊ ❊ ❊ ❊ ❊ ❊ ❊ ❊ ❊

JESUS CLEANSES THE TEMPLE
Mark 11

15

So they came to Jerusalem. Then Jesus went into the temple and began to drive out those who bought and sold in the temple, and overturned the tables of the money changers and the seats of those who sold doves.

16

And He would not allow anyone to carry wares through the temple.

17

Then He taught, saying to them, "Is it not written, 'My house shall be called a house of prayer for all nations'? But you have made it a den of thieves.' "

18

And the scribes and chief priests heard it and sought how they might destroy Him; for they feared Him, because all the people were astonished at His teaching.

Tuesday

MARY ANOINTS JESUS AT BETHANY
Mark 14

3

And being in Bethany at the house of Simon the leper, as He sat at the table, a woman came having an alabaster flask of very costly oil of spikenard. Then she broke the flask and poured it on His head.

4

But there were some who were indig-
nant among themselves, and said,
"Why was this fragrant oil wasted?

5

"For it might have been sold for more
than three hundred denarii and
given to the poor." And they criti-
cized her sharply.

6

*But Jesus said, "Let her alone. Why
do you trouble her? She has done a
good work for Me.*

7

*"For you have the poor with you
always, and whenever you wish you
may do them good; but Me you do
not have always.*

8

"She has done what she could. She

❀ ❀ ❀ ❀ ❀ ❀ ❀ ❀ ❀ ❀ ❀ ❀ ❀ ❀ ❀

has come beforehand to anoint My body for burial.

9

"Assuredly, I say to you, wherever this gospel is preached in the whole world, what this woman has done will also be told as a memorial to her."

JUDAS CONTRACTS TO BETRAY JESUS
Luke 22

1

Now the Feast of Unleavened Bread drew near, which is called Passover.

2

And the chief priests and the scribes sought how they might kill Him, for they feared the people.

3

Then Satan entered Judas, surnamed Iscariot, who was numbered among the twelve.

4

So he went his way and conferred with the chief priests and captains, how he might betray Him to them.

5

And they were glad, and agreed to give him money.

6

So he promised and sought opportunity to betray Him to them in the absence of the multitude.

Thursday

PREPARATION FOR
THE PASSOVER
Luke 22

7

Then came the Day of Unleavened Bread, when the Passover must be killed.

8

And He sent Peter and John, saying, "Go and prepare the Passover for us, that we may eat."

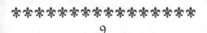

9

So they said to Him, "Where do You want us to prepare?"

10

And He said to them, "Behold, when you have entered the city, a man will meet you carrying a pitcher of water; follow him into the house which he enters.

11

"Then you shall say to the master of

❄ ❄ ❄ ❄ ❄ ❄ ❄ ❄ ❄ ❄ ❄ ❄ ❄ ❄ ❄

the house, 'The Teacher says to you, "Where is the guest room where I may eat the Passover with My disciples?"'

12

"Then he will show you a large, furnished upper room; there make ready."

13

So they went and found it just as He had said to them, and they prepared the Passover.

JESUS CELEBRATES THE PASSOVER WITH HIS DISCIPLES
John 13

1
Now before the Feast of the Passover, when Jesus knew that His hour had come that He should depart from this world to the Father, having loved His own who were in the world, He loved them to the end.

❄ ❄ ❄ ❄ ❄ ❄ ❄ ❄ ❄ ❄ ❄ ❄ ❄ ❄

2

And supper being ended, the devil having already put it into the heart of Judas Iscariot, Simon's son, to betray Him,

3

Jesus, knowing that the Father had given all things into His hands, and that He had come from God and was going to God,

4

rose from supper and laid aside His

❀ ❀ ❀ ❀ ❀ ❀ ❀ ❀ ❀ ❀ ❀ ❀ ❀ ❀ ❀

garments, took a towel and girded Himself.

5

After that, He poured water into a basin and began to wash the disciples' feet, and to wipe them with the towel with which He was girded.

6

Then He came to Simon Peter. And Peter said to Him, "Lord, are You washing my feet?"

❊ ❊ ❊ ❊ ❊ ❊ ❊ ❊ ❊ ❊ ❊ ❊ ❊ ❊ ❊

7

Jesus answered and said to him, "What I am doing you do not understand now, but you will know after this."

8

Peter said to Him, "You shall never wash my feet!" Jesus answered him, "If I do not wash you, you have no part with Me."

9

Simon Peter said to Him, "Lord, not

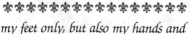

my feet only, but also my hands and my head!''

10

Jesus said to him, ''He who is bathed needs only to wash his feet, but is completely clean; and you are clean, but not all of you.''

11

For He knew who would betray Him; therefore He said, ''You are not all clean.''

❀ ❀ ❀ ❀ ❀ ❀ ❀ ❀ ❀ ❀ ❀ ❀ ❀ ❀ ❀

12

So when He had washed their feet, taken His garments, and sat down again, He said to them, "Do you know what I have done to you?

13

"You call Me Teacher and Lord, and you say well, for so I am.

14

"If I then, your Lord and Teacher,

❄ ❄ ❄ ❄ ❄ ❄ ❄ ❄ ❄ ❄ ❄ ❄ ❄ ❄ ❄

have washed your feet, you also ought to wash one another's feet.

15

"For I have given you an example, that you should do as I have done to you.

16

"Most assuredly, I say to you, a servant is not greater than his master;

❊ ❊ ❊ ❊ ❊ ❊ ❊ ❊ ❊ ❊ ❊ ❊ ❊ ❊

nor is he who is sent greater than he who sent him.

17

"If you know these things, blessed are you if you do them.

18

"I do not speak concerning all of you. I know whom I have chosen; but that the Scripture may be fulfilled, 'He who eats bread with Me has lifted up his heel against Me.'

❋ ❋ ❋ ❋ ❋ ❋ ❋ ❋ ❋ ❋ ❋ ❋ ❋ ❋ ❋

19

"Now I tell you before it comes, that when it does come to pass, you may believe that I am He.

20

"Most assuredly, I say to you, he who receives whomever I send receives Me; and he who receives Me receives Him who sent Me."

21

When Jesus had said these things,

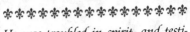

He was troubled in spirit, and testified and said, "Most assuredly, I say to you, one of you will betray Me."

22

Then the disciples looked at one another, perplexed about whom He spoke.

23

Now there was leaning on Jesus' bosom one of His disciples, whom Jesus loved.

�֎ �֎ ✾ ✾ ✾ ✾ ✾ ✾ ✾ ✾ ✾ ✾ ✾ ✾ ✾ ✾

24

Simon Peter therefore motioned to him to ask who it was of whom He spoke.

25

Then, leaning back on Jesus' breast, he said to Him, "Lord, who is it?"

26

Jesus answered, "It is he to whom I shall give a piece of bread when I have dipped it." And having dipped

❧ ❧ ❧ ❧ ❧ ❧ ❧ ❧ ❧ ❧ ❧ ❧ ❧ ❧ ❧

the bread, He gave it to Judas Iscariot, the son of Simon.

27

Now after the piece of bread, Satan entered him. Then Jesus said to him, "What you do, do quickly."

28

But no one at the table knew for what reason He said this to him.

29

For some thought, because Judas had

❀ ❀ ❀ ❀ ❀ ❀ ❀ ❀ ❀ ❀ ❀ ❀ ❀ ❀ ❀

the money box, that Jesus had said to him, "Buy those things we need for the feast," or that he should give something to the poor.

30

Having received the piece of bread, he then went out immediately. And it was night.

31

So, when he had gone out, Jesus said,

❊ ❊ ❊ ❊ ❊ ❊ ❊ ❊ ❊ ❊ ❊ ❊ ❊ ❊

"Now the Son of Man is glorified,
and God is glorified in Him.

32

"If God is glorified in Him, God will
also glorify Him in Himself, and glorify Him immediately.

33

"Little children, I shall be with you
a little while longer. You will seek
Me; and as I said to the Jews,

❊ ❊ ❊ ❊ ❊ ❊ ❊ ❊ ❊ ❊ ❊ ❊ ❊ ❊ ❊

'Where I am going, you cannot come,' so now I say to you.

34

"A new commandment I give to you, that you love one another; as I have loved you, that you also love one another.

35

"By this all will know that you are My disciples, if you have love for one another."

36

Simon Peter said to Him, "Lord, where are You going?" Jesus answered him, "Where I am going you cannot follow Me now, but you shall follow Me afterward."

37

Peter said to Him, "Lord, why can I not follow You now? I will lay down my life for Your sake."

❄ ❄ ❄ ❄ ❄ ❄ ❄ ❄ ❄ ❄ ❄ ❄ ❄ ❄ ❄ ❄

38

Jesus answered him, "Will you lay down your life for My sake? Most assuredly, I say to you, the rooster shall not crow till you have denied Me three times."

THE LORD'S SUPPER
INSTITUTED
Luke 22

14

When the hour had come, He sat down, and the twelve apostles with Him.

15

Then He said to them, "With fervent desire I have desired to eat this Passover with you before I suffer;

❊ ❊ ❊ ❊ ❊ ❊ ❊ ❊ ❊ ❊ ❊ ❊ ❊ ❊ ❊

16

"for I say to you, I will no longer eat of it until it is fulfilled in the kingdom of God."

17

Then He took the cup, and gave thanks, and said, "Take this and divide it among yourselves;

18

"for I say to you, I will not drink of the fruit of the vine until the kingdom of God comes."

19

And He took bread, gave thanks and broke it, and gave it to them, saying, "This is My body which is given for you; do this in remembrance of Me."

20

Likewise He also took the cup after supper, saying, "This cup is the new covenant in My blood, which is shed for you."

✿ ✿ ✿ ✿ ✿ ✿ ✿ ✿ ✿ ✿ ✿ ✿ ✿ ✿

JESUS PRAYS BEFORE HIS ARREST
John 17

1

Jesus spoke these words, lifted up His eyes to heaven, and said: "Father, the hour has come. Glorify Your Son, that Your Son also may glorify You,

2

"as You have given Him authority over all flesh, that He should give

❀ ❀ ❀ ❀ ❀ ❀ ❀ ❀ ❀ ❀ ❀ ❀ ❀ ❀ ❀

eternal life to as many as You have given Him.

3

"And this is eternal life, that they may know You, the only true God, and Jesus Christ whom You have sent.

4

"I have glorified You on the earth. I have finished the work which You have given Me to do.

5

"And now, O Father, glorify Me together with Yourself, with the glory which I had with You before the world was.

6

"I have manifested Your name to the men whom You have given Me out of the world. They were Yours, You gave them to Me, and they have kept Your word.

❧ ❧ ❧ ❧ ❧ ❧ ❧ ❧ ❧ ❧ ❧ ❧ ❧ ❧ ❧

7

"Now they have known that all things which You have given Me are from You.

8

"For I have given to them the words which You have given Me; and they have received them, and have known surely that I came forth from You; and they have believed that You sent Me.

❀ ❀ ❀ ❀ ❀ ❀ ❀ ❀ ❀ ❀ ❀ ❀ ❀ ❀ ❀ ❀

9

"I pray for them. I do not pray for the world but for those whom You have given Me, for they are Yours.

10

"And all Mine are Yours, and Yours are Mine, and I am glorified in them.

11

"Now I am no longer in the world, but these are in the world, and I

❀ ❀ ❀ ❀ ❀ ❀ ❀ ❀ ❀ ❀ ❀ ❀ ❀ ❀ ❀

come to You. Holy Father, keep
through Your name those whom You
have given Me, that they may be one
as We are.

12

"While I was with them in the
world, I kept them in Your name.
Those whom You gave Me I have
kept; and none of them is lost except
the son of perdition, that the Scripture might be fulfilled.

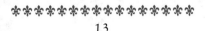

13

"But now I come to You, and these things I speak in the world, that they may have My joy fulfilled in themselves.

14

"I have given them Your word; and the world has hated them because they are not of the world, just as I am not of the world.

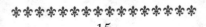

15

"I do not pray that You should take them out of the world, but that You should keep them from the evil one.

16

"They are not of the world, just as I am not of the world.

17

"Sanctify them by Your truth. Your word is truth.

❊ ❊ ❊ ❊ ❊ ❊ ❊ ❊ ❊ ❊ ❊ ❊ ❊ ❊ ❊

18

"As You sent Me into the world, I also have sent them into the world.

19

"And for their sakes I sanctify Myself, that they also may be sanctified by the truth.

20

"I do not pray for these alone, but also for those who will believe in Me through their word;

❀ ❀ ❀ ❀ ❀ ❀ ❀ ❀ ❀ ❀ ❀ ❀ ❀ ❀ ❀

21

"that they all may be one, as You, Father, are in Me, and I in You; that they also may be one in Us, that the world may believe that You sent Me.

22

"And the glory which You gave Me I have given them, that they may be one just as We are one:

23

"I in them, and You in Me; that

they may be made perfect in one, and that the world may know that You have sent Me, and have loved them as You have loved Me.

24

"Father, I desire that they also whom You gave Me may be with Me where I am, that they may behold My glory which You have given Me; for You loved Me before the foundation of the world.

❀ ❀ ❀ ❀ ❀ ❀ ❀ ❀ ❀ ❀ ❀ ❀ ❀ ❀ ❀

25

"O righteous Father! The world has not known You, but I have known You; and these have known that You sent Me.

26

"And I have declared to them Your name, and will declare it, that the love with which You loved Me may be in them, and I in them."

Friday

BETRAYAL, ARREST, AND DESERTION

Mark 14

32

Then they came to a place which was named Gethsemane; and He said to His disciples, "Sit here while I pray."

33

And He took Peter, James, and John

❋ ❋ ❋ ❋ ❋ ❋ ❋ ❋ ❋ ❋ ❋ ❋ ❋ ❋ ❋

with Him, and He began to be troubled and deeply distressed.

34

Then He said to them, "My soul is exceedingly sorrowful, even to death. Stay here and watch."

35

He went a little farther, and fell on the ground, and prayed that if it were possible, the hour might pass from Him.

36

And He said, "Abba, Father, all things are possible for You. Take this cup away from Me; nevertheless, not what I will, but what You will."

37

Then He came and found them sleeping, and said to Peter, "Simon, are you sleeping? Could you not watch one hour?

38

"Watch and pray, lest you enter into

temptation. The spirit indeed is willing, but the flesh is weak."

39

Again He went away and prayed, and spoke the same words.

40

And when He returned, He found them asleep again, for their eyes were heavy; and they did not know what to answer Him.

❖ ❖ ❖ ❖ ❖ ❖ ❖ ❖ ❖ ❖ ❖ ❖ ❖ ❖

41

Then He came the third time and said to them, "Are you still sleeping and resting? It is enough! The hour has come; behold, the Son of Man is being betrayed into the hands of sinners.

42

"Rise, let us be going. See, My betrayer is at hand."

43

And immediately, while He was still speaking, Judas, one of the twelve, with a great multitude with swords and clubs, came from the chief priests and the scribes and the elders.

44

Now His betrayer had given them a signal, saying, "Whomever I kiss, He is the One; seize Him and lead Him away safely."

45

As soon as He had come, immediately he went up to Him and said to Him, "Rabbi, Rabbi!" and kissed Him.

46

Then they laid their hands on Him and took Him.

47

And one of those who stood by drew his sword and struck the servant of

❄ ❄ ❄ ❄ ❄ ❄ ❄ ❄ ❄ ❄ ❄ ❄ ❄ ❄ ❄ ❄

the high priest, and cut off his ear.

48

Then Jesus answered and said to them, "Have you come out, as against a robber, with swords and clubs to take Me?

49

"I was daily with you in the temple teaching, and you did not seize Me. But the Scriptures must be fulfilled."

50

Then they all forsook Him and fled.

51

Now a certain young man followed Him, having a linen cloth thrown around his naked body. And the young men laid hold of him,

52

and he left the linen cloth and fled from them naked.

❁ ❁ ❁ ❁ ❁ ❁ ❁ ❁ ❁ ❁ ❁ ❁ ❁ ❁ ❁

ANNAS QUESTIONS JESUS
John 18

12

Then the detachment of troops and the captain and the officers of the Jews arrested Jesus and bound Him.

13

And they led Him away to Annas first, for he was the father-in-law of Caiaphas who was high priest that year.

❀ ❀ ❀ ❀ ❀ ❀ ❀ ❀ ❀ ❀ ❀ ❀ ❀ ❀ ❀

14

Now it was Caiaphas who advised the Jews that it was expedient that one man should die for the people.

* * *

19

The high priest then asked Jesus about His disciples and His doctrine.

20

Jesus answered him, "I spoke openly

❧ ❧ ❧ ❧ ❧ ❧ ❧ ❧ ❧ ❧ ❧ ❧ ❧ ❧ ❧ ❧

to the world. I always taught in synagogues and in the temple, where the Jews always meet, and in secret I have said nothing.

21

"Why do you ask Me? Ask those who have heard Me what I said to them. Indeed they know what I said."

22

And when He had said these things,

❀ ❀ ❀ ❀ ❀ ❀ ❀ ❀ ❀ ❀ ❀ ❀ ❀ ❀ ❀

one of the officers who stood by struck Jesus with the palm of his hand, saying, "Do You answer the high priest like that?"

23

Jesus answered him, "If I have spoken evil, bear witness of the evil; but if well, why do you strike Me?"

24

Then Annas sent Him bound to Caiaphas the high priest.

❀ ❀ ❀ ❀ ❀ ❀ ❀ ❀ ❀ ❀ ❀ ❀ ❀ ❀ ❀

TRIAL BY CAIAPHAS AND THE SANHEDRIN
Mark 14

53

And they led Jesus away to the high priest; and with him were assembled all the chief priests, the elders, and the scribes.

54

But Peter followed Him at a distance, right into the courtyard of the high

✳ ✳ ✳ ✳ ✳ ✳ ✳ ✳ ✳ ✳ ✳ ✳ ✳ ✳ ✳ ✳

*priest. And he sat with the servants
and warmed himself at the fire.*

55

*Now the chief priests and all the
council sought testimony against
Jesus to put Him to death, but found
none.*

56

*For many bore false witness against
Him, but their testimonies did not
agree.*

57

Then some rose up and bore false witness against Him, saying,

58

"We heard Him say, 'I will destroy this temple made with hands, and within three days I will build another made without hands.'"

59

But not even then did their testimony agree.

60

And the high priest stood up in the midst and asked Jesus, saying, "Do You answer nothing? What is it these men testify against You?"

61

But He kept silent and answered nothing. Again the high priest asked Him, saying to Him, "Are You the Christ, the Son of the Blessed?"

62

Jesus said, "I am. And you will see the Son of Man sitting at the right hand of the Power, and coming with the clouds of heaven."

63

Then the high priest tore his clothes and said, "What further need do we have of witnesses?

✤ ✤ ✤ ✤ ✤ ✤ ✤ ✤ ✤ ✤ ✤ ✤ ✤ ✤ ✤ ✤

64

"You have heard the blasphemy! What do you think?" And they all condemned Him to be deserving of death.

65

Then some began to spit on Him, and to blindfold Him, and to beat Him, and to say to Him, "Prophesy!" And the officers struck Him with the palms of their hands.

❀ ❀ ❀ ❀ ❀ ❀ ❀ ❀ ❀ ❀ ❀ ❀ ❀ ❀ ❀

PETER DENIES JESUS
John 18

15

And Simon Peter followed Jesus, and so did another disciple. Now that disciple was known to the high priest, and went with Jesus into the courtyard of the high priest.

16

But Peter stood at the door outside. Then the other disciple, who was

❀ ❀ ❀ ❀ ❀ ❀ ❀ ❀ ❀ ❀ ❀ ❀ ❀ ❀ ❀

known to the high priest, went out
and spoke to her who kept the door,
and brought Peter in.

17

Then the servant girl who kept the
door said to Peter, "You are not also
one of this Man's disciples, are you?"
He said, "I am not."

18

Now the servants and officers who
had made a fire of coals stood there,

for it was cold, and they warmed
themselves. And Peter stood with
them and warmed himself.

* * *

25

Now Simon Peter stood and warmed
himself. Therefore they said to him,
"You are not also one of His disciples, are you?" He denied it and said,
"I am not!"

26

One of the servants of the high priest, a relative of him whose ear Peter cut off, said, "Did I not see you in the garden with Him?"

27

Peter then denied again; and immediately a rooster crowed.

✾ ✾ ✾ ✾ ✾ ✾ ✾ ✾ ✾ ✾ ✾ ✾ ✾ ✾ ✾

THE SANHEDRIN
FORMALLY
CONDEMNS JESUS
Luke 22

66

As soon as it was day, the elders of the people, both chief priests and scribes, came together and led Him into their council, saying,

67

"If You are the Christ, tell us." But

He said to them, "If I tell you, you will by no means believe.

68

"And if I also ask you, you will by no means answer Me or let Me go.

69

"Hereafter the Son of Man will sit on the right hand of the power of God."

70

Then they all said, "Are You then

✤ ✤ ✤ ✤ ✤ ✤ ✤ ✤ ✤ ✤ ✤ ✤ ✤ ✤ ✤

the Son of God?" So He said to them, "You rightly say that I am."

71

And they said, "What further testimony do we need? For we have heard it ourselves from His own mouth."

JUDAS COMMITS SUICIDE
Matthew 27

1

When morning came, all the chief priests and elders of the people plotted against Jesus to put Him to death.

2

And when they had bound Him, they led Him away and delivered Him to Pontius Pilate the governor.

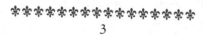

3

Then Judas, His betrayer, seeing that He had been condemned, was remorseful and brought back the thirty pieces of silver to the chief priests and elders,

4

saying, "I have sinned by betraying innocent blood." And they said, "What is that to us? You see to it!"

❊ ❊ ❊ ❊ ❊ ❊ ❊ ❊ ❊ ❊ ❊ ❊ ❊ ❊ ❊ ❊

5

Then he threw down the pieces of silver in the temple and departed, and went and hanged himself.

6

But the chief priests took the silver pieces and said, "It is not lawful to put them into the treasury, because they are the price of blood."

7

And they consulted together and

❧ ❧ ❧ ❧ ❧ ❧ ❧ ❧ ❧ ❧ ❧ ❧ ❧ ❧ ❧

bought with them the potter's field, to bury strangers in.

8

Therefore that field has been called the Field of Blood to this day.

9

Then was fulfilled what was spoken by Jeremiah the prophet, saying, "And they took the thirty pieces of silver, the value of Him who was

❀ ❀ ❀ ❀ ❀ ❀ ❀ ❀ ❀ ❀ ❀ ❀ ❀ ❀ ❀ ❀

priced, whom they of the children of
Israel priced,

10

"and gave them for the potter's field,
as the LORD directed me."

❀ ❀ ❀ ❀ ❀ ❀ ❀ ❀ ❀ ❀ ❀ ❀ ❀ ❀ ❀

JESUS BEFORE PILATE
AND HEROD
Luke 23

1

Then the whole multitude of them
arose and led Him to Pilate.

2

And they began to accuse Him, saying, "We found this fellow pervert-
ing the nation, and forbidding to

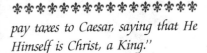

pay taxes to Caesar, saying that He Himself is Christ, a King."

3

Then Pilate asked Him, saying, "Are You the King of the Jews?" He answered him and said, "It is as you say."

4

So Pilate said to the chief priests and the crowd, "I find no fault in this Man."

5

But they were the more fierce, saying, "He stirs up the people, teaching throughout all Judea, beginning from Galilee to this place."

6

When Pilate heard of Galilee, he asked if the Man were a Galilean.

7

And as soon as he knew that He belonged to Herod's jurisdiction, he

❉ ❉ ❉ ❉ ❉ ❉ ❉ ❉ ❉ ❉ ❉ ❉ ❉ ❉ ❉

sent Him to Herod, who was also in Jerusalem at that time.

8

Now when Herod saw Jesus, he was exceedingly glad; for he had desired for a long time to see Him, because he had heard many things about Him, and he hoped to see some miracle done by Him.

9

Then he questioned Him with many

❀ ❀ ❀ ❀ ❀ ❀ ❀ ❀ ❀ ❀ ❀ ❀ ❀ ❀ ❀

words, but He answered him nothing.

10

And the chief priests and scribes stood and vehemently accused Him.

11

Then Herod, with his men of war, treated Him with contempt and mocked Him, arrayed Him in a gorgeous robe, and sent Him back to Pilate.

12

That very day Pilate and Herod became friends with each other, for previously they had been at enmity with each other.

13

Then Pilate, when he had called together the chief priests, the rulers, and the people,

14

said to them, "You have brought this

Man to me, as one who misleads the people. And indeed, having examined Him in your presence, I have found no fault in this Man concerning those things of which you accuse Him;

15

"no, neither did Herod, for I sent you back to him; and indeed nothing deserving of death has been done by Him.

16

"I will therefore chastise Him and release Him"

17

(for it was necessary for him to release one to them at the feast).

18

And they all cried out at once, saying, "Away with this Man, and release to us Barabbas"—

19

who had been thrown into prison for a certain rebellion made in the city, and for murder.

20

Pilate, therefore, wishing to release Jesus, again called out to them.

21

But they shouted, saying, "Crucify Him, crucify Him!"

❀ ❀ ❀ ❀ ❀ ❀ ❀ ❀ ❀ ❀ ❀ ❀ ❀ ❀

22

Then he said to them the third time, "Why, what evil has He done? I have found no reason for death in Him. I will therefore chastise Him and let Him go."

23

But they were insistent, demanding with loud voices that He be crucified. And the voices of these men and of the chief priests prevailed.

24

So Pilate gave sentence that it should be as they requested.

25

And he released to them the one they requested, who for rebellion and murder had been thrown into prison; but he delivered Jesus to their will.

JESUS MOCKED
AND CRUCIFIED
Mark 15

16

Then the soldiers led Him away into the hall called Praetorium, and they called together the whole garrison.

17

And they clothed Him with purple; and they twisted a crown of thorns, put it on His head,

18

and began to salute Him, "Hail, King of the Jews!"

19

Then they struck Him on the head with a reed and spat on Him; and bowing the knee, they worshiped Him.

20

And when they had mocked Him, they took the purple off Him, put His

✤ ✤ ✤ ✤ ✤ ✤ ✤ ✤ ✤ ✤ ✤ ✤ ✤ ✤ ✤

*own clothes on Him, and led Him
out to crucify Him.*

21

*Then they compelled a certain man,
Simon a Cyrenian, the father of
Alexander and Rufus, as he was
coming out of the country and
passing by, to bear His cross.*

22

And they brought Him to the place

✤ ✤ ✤ ✤ ✤ ✤ ✤ ✤ ✤ ✤ ✤ ✤ ✤ ✤ ✤

Golgotha, which is translated, Place of a Skull.

23

Then they gave Him wine mingled with myrrh to drink, but He did not take it.

24

And when they crucified Him, they divided His garments, casting lots for them to determine what every man should take.

25

Now it was the third hour, and they crucified Him.

26

And the inscription of His accusation was written above:

THE KING OF THE JEWS.

27

With Him they also crucified two robbers, one on His right and the other on His left.

28

So the Scripture was fulfilled which says, "And He was numbered with the transgressors."

29

And those who passed by blasphemed Him, wagging their heads and saying, "Aha! You who destroy the temple and build it in three days,

30

"save Yourself, and come down from the cross!"

❧ ❧ ❧ ❧ ❧ ❧ ❧ ❧ ❧ ❧ ❧ ❧ ❧ ❧ ❧ ❧

31

Likewise the chief priests also, mocking among themselves with the scribes, said, "He saved others; Himself He cannot save.

32

"Let the Christ, the King of Israel, descend now from the cross, that we may see and believe." Even those who were crucified with Him reviled Him.

❀ ❀ ❀ ❀ ❀ ❀ ❀ ❀ ❀ ❀ ❀ ❀ ❀ ❀

BEHOLD YOUR MOTHER
John 19

25

Now there stood by the cross of Jesus His mother, and His mother's sister, Mary the wife of Clopas, and Mary Magdalene.

26

When Jesus therefore saw His mother, and the disciple whom He

❊ ❊ ❊ ❊ ❊ ❊ ❊ ❊ ❊ ❊ ❊ ❊ ❊ ❊ ❊

loved standing by, He said to His mother, "Woman, behold your son!"

27

Then He said to the disciple, "Behold your mother!" And from that hour that disciple took her to his own home.

❁ ❁ ❁ ❁ ❁ ❁ ❁ ❁ ❁ ❁ ❁ ❁ ❁ ❁ ❁

JESUS DIES ON THE CROSS
Matthew 27

45

Now from the sixth hour until the ninth hour there was darkness over all the land.

46

And about the ninth hour Jesus cried out with a loud voice, saying, "Eli, Eli, lama sabachthani?" that is,

"My God, My God, why have You forsaken Me?"

47

Some of those who stood there, when they heard that, said, "This Man is calling for Elijah!"

48

Immediately one of them ran and took a sponge, filled it with sour wine and put it on a reed, and offered it to Him to drink.

49

The rest said, "Let Him alone; let us see if Elijah will come to save Him."

50

And Jesus cried out again with a loud voice, and yielded up His spirit.

51

Then, behold, the veil of the temple was torn in two from top to bottom; and the earth quaked, and the rocks were split,

52

and the graves were opened; and many bodies of the saints who had fallen asleep were raised;

53

and coming out of the graves after His resurrection, they went into the holy city and appeared to many.

54

So when the centurion and those with him, who were guarding Jesus,

saw the earthquake and the things that had happened, they feared greatly, saying, "Truly this was the Son of God!"

55

And many women who followed Jesus from Galilee, ministering to Him, were there looking on from afar,

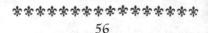

56

among whom were Mary Magdalene, Mary the mother of James and
Joses, and the mother of Zebedee's
sons.

❧ ❧ ❧ ❧ ❧ ❧ ❧ ❧ ❧ ❧ ❧ ❧ ❧ ❧ ❧

THE BURIAL OF JESUS
John 19

31

Therefore, because it was the Preparation Day, that the bodies should not remain on the cross on the Sabbath (for that Sabbath was a high day), the Jews asked Pilate that their legs might be broken, and that they might be taken away.

32

Then the soldiers came and broke the legs of the first and of the other who was crucified with Him.

33

But when they came to Jesus and saw that He was already dead, they did not break His legs.

34

But one of the soldiers pierced His

✿ ✿ ✿ ✿ ✿ ✿ ✿ ✿ ✿ ✿ ✿ ✿ ✿ ✿ ✿

side with a spear, and immediately blood and water came out.

35

And he who has seen has testified, and his testimony is true; and he knows that he is telling the truth, so that you may believe.

36

For these things were done that the Scripture should be fulfilled, "Not one of His bones shall be broken."

37

And again another Scripture says, "They shall look on Him whom they pierced."

38

After this, Joseph of Arimathea, being a disciple of Jesus, but secretly, for fear of the Jews, asked Pilate that he might take away the body of Jesus; and Pilate gave him permission. So he came and took the body of Jesus.

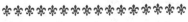

39

And Nicodemus, who at first came to Jesus by night, also came, bringing a mixture of myrrh and aloes, about a hundred pounds.

40

Then they took the body of Jesus, and bound it in strips of linen with the spices, as the custom of the Jews is to bury.

✳ ✳ ✳ ✳ ✳ ✳ ✳ ✳ ✳ ✳ ✳ ✳ ✳ ✳ ✳

41

Now in the place where He was crucified there was a garden, and in the garden a new tomb in which no one had yet been laid.

42

So there they laid Jesus, because of the Jews' Preparation Day, for the tomb was nearby.

Sunday

HE IS RISEN!
Matthew 28

1

Now after the Sabbath, as the first day of the week began to dawn, Mary Magdalene and the other Mary came to see the tomb.

2

And behold, there was a great earthquake; for an angel of the Lord descended from heaven, and came and

✿ ✿ ✿ ✿ ✿ ✿ ✿ ✿ ✿ ✿ ✿ ✿ ✿ ✿ ✿

rolled back the stone from the door,
and sat on it.

3

His countenance was like lightning,
and his clothing as white as snow.

4

And the guards shook for fear of
him, and became like dead men.

5

But the angel answered and said to
the women, "Do not be afraid, for I

❧ ❧ ❧ ❧ ❧ ❧ ❧ ❧ ❧ ❧ ❧ ❧ ❧ ❧ ❧

know that you seek Jesus who was crucified.

6

"He is not here; for He is risen, as He said. Come, see the place where the Lord lay.

7

"And go quickly and tell His disciples that He is risen from the dead, and indeed He is going before you into Galilee; there you will see Him. Behold, I have told you."